Pebble®
Plus

Creepy Crawlers

Millipedes

by Nikki Bruno Clapper

Gail Saunders-Smith, PhD, Consulting Editor

Consultant: Orin A. McMonigle
Editor in Chief
Invertebrates Magazine

CAPSTONE PRESS
a capstone imprint

Pebble Plus is published by Capstone Press,
1710 Roe Crest Drive, North Mankato, Minnesota 56003.
www.capstonepub.com

Library of Congress Cataloging-in-Publication Data
Clapper, Nikki Bruno, author.
Millipedes/by Nikki Bruno Clapper.
pages cm.—(Pebble Plus. Creepy Crawlers)
Summary: "Simple text and full-color photographs introduce
millipedes"—Provided by publisher.
Audience: Ages 4–8.
Audience: K to grade 3.
Includes bibliographical references and index.
ISBN 978-1-4914-6214-0 (library binding)
ISBN 978-1-4914-6226-3 (eBook PDF)
1. Millipedes—Juvenile literature. I. Title. II. Series: Pebble Plus.
Creepy crawlers.
QL449.6.C53 2016
595.6'6—dc23   2015008506

Editorial Credits
Michelle Bisson and Jeni Wittrock, editors; Juliette Peters, designer; Katy LaVigne, production specialist

Photo Credits
James P. Rowan, 5, 9, 15; Newscom: Minden Pictures/Mark Moffett, 21, Minden Pictures/Plotr Naskreckl, 7, Photoshot/ NHPA/James Carmichael Jr, 13; Science Source: Danté Fenolio, 19; Shutterstock: BENZINE, 1, JoeFotoSS, 17, kamnuan, cover; SuperStock: NHPA, 11

Design Element
Shutterstock: vlastas66

Note to Parents and Teachers

The Creepy Crawlers set supports national science standards related to biology and life science. This book describes and illustrates millipedes. The images support early readers in understanding the text. The repetition of words and phrases helps early readers learn new words. This book also introduces early readers to subject-specific vocabulary words, which are defined in the Glossary section. Early readers may need assistance to read some words and to use the Table of Contents, Glossary, Read More, Critical Thinking Using the Common Core, Internet Sites, and Index sections of the book.

Printed in the United States of America in North Mankato, Minnesota.
042015   008823CGF15

Table of Contents

Slow but Scary

A long, skinny creature

crawls out from under a log.

Its creepy legs move slowly.

It must have 100 legs!

This creature is a millipede.

Millipedes are arthropods.

An arthropod's body is split

into parts called segments.

segments

Damp, Dark Places

Millipedes live in dark, damp places all around the world. They hide under rocks, logs, and leaves. A millipede dies if it gets too dry.

A Millipede's Body

A millipede's body is covered with a smooth, hard exoskeleton. The creature breathes through tiny holes called spiracles.

exoskeleton

Most millipede segments have four legs each. The total leg count can be 36 to 750. Some millipedes are longer than 1 foot (31 centimeters)!

giant African millipede

Ground Chompers

Most millipedes are nocturnal. That means they are active at night. In the darkness they chomp on rotting plants and fungi.

Stopping Predators

Frogs, birds, and lizards eat millipedes. If a predator gets close, the millipede rolls into a coil. This shape protects its head and legs.

Most millipedes stay safe by letting out a stinky liquid. Some millipedes glow in the dark. Predators know these glowing bugs have poison.

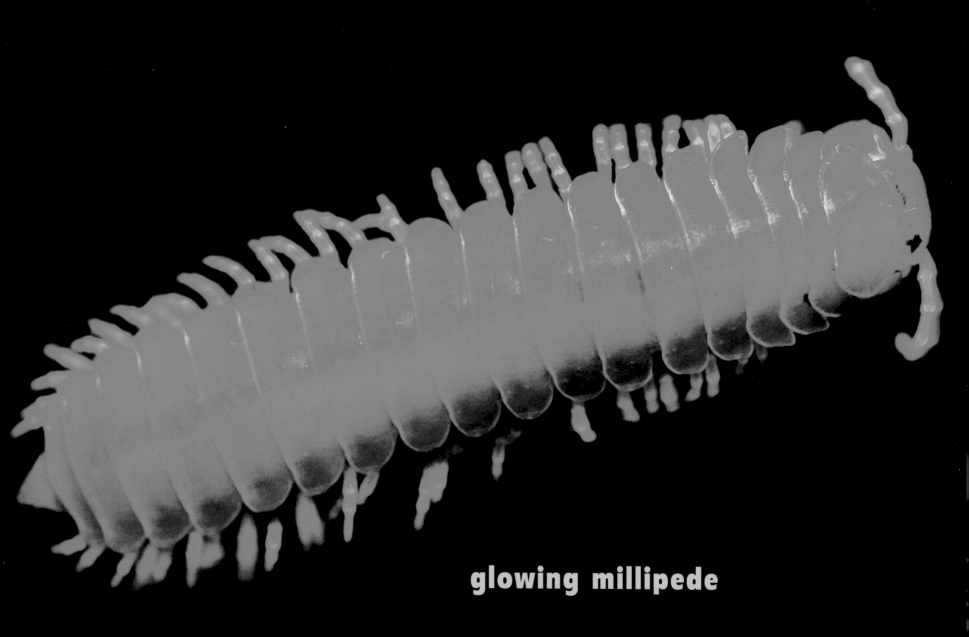

glowing millipede

The **Millipede Life**

Female millipedes lay eggs.
After three to four weeks, baby
millipedes hatch from the eggs.
They grow segments. Millipedes
live for up to 15 years.

Glossary

arthropod—an animal with a hard outer shell and many legs with joints

damp—slightly wet

exoskeleton—the hard outer shell of an arthropod; the exoskeleton covers and protects the animal

fungi—a type of organism that has no leaves, flowers, or roots

hatch—to break out of an egg

nocturnal—active at night and resting during the day

poison—a substance that can harm or kill an animal or person

predator—an animal that hunts other animals for food

segment—one of the pieces that makes up an arthropod's body

spiracle—an opening on a millipede's body through which it breathes

warn—to tell about a danger that might happen in the future

Read More

Creepy-Crawlies: A 3D Pocket Guide. Somerville, Mass.: Candlewick Press, 2013.

Hughes, Catherine D. *Little Kids First Big Book of Bugs.* Washington, D.C.: National Geographic Society, 2014.

Rockwood, Leigh. *Centipedes and Millipedes Are Gross!* Creepy Crawlies. New York: PowerKids Press, 2011.

Internet Sites

FactHound offers a safe, fun way to find Internet sites related to this book. All of the sites on FactHound have been researched by our staff.

Here's all you do:

Visit *www.facthound.com*

Type in this code: 9781491462140

Super-cool stuff!

Check out projects, games and lots more at
www.capstonekids.com

Critical Thinking
Using the Common Core

1. When would a millipede roll up into a coil? How does coiling help protect millipedes? (Key Ideas and Details)

2. What might happen if there were no millipedes to eat rotting plants and fungi? (Integration of Knowledge and Ideas)

Index

Word Count: 196
Grade: 1
Early-Intervention Level: 19